Possible connections between Indigen⸤ languages and languages elsewhere, w reference to Quechuan languages, and w⸤ on elongated skulls, pyramids, giants and other philosophical points

Written by Linden Alexander Pentecost, published by Linden Alexander Pentecost on the 8th of April 2023, re-uploaded on the 22nnd of April with some final changes, although the publication date is the 8th. Published via Amazon from the UK, I, the author am a UK resident.
Proofreading by Daryn Akei Melvin, who also made some edits to make the text clearer, and to more accurately word some of the things about Hopi history, Daryn is himself Hopi.

Note: this book contains some topics of symbolism, which, although metaphysical, symbolic, and discussed analytically, may be unsuitable for younger audiences (those under 18).

Internal photo of Signal Hill in Arizona also by Linden Alexander Pentecost. Front cover photo by Linden Alexander Pentecost, this photo shows a landscape in Arizona with pine forests and skies, I include this photo because it reminds me a bit of the pine forests in Finland, and with pine tree landscapes themselves being so ancient, I feel that, like pine trees, ancient things in different parts of the World, and like the clouds across the world, perhaps some of our words in languages are similar, hence the choice of this photo for the front cover photo.
The word connections in this book and other information are mostly what I have noticed recently.
This book contains 31 internal pages (not including the front and back cover pages and their inside or possible blank pages after them for example), this is page one, the contents is on page 2. Page number is indicated in all four corners of page. The font size in the main body of text (not references, titles or these paragraphs, footnotes, the Signal Hill photo description, the final notes section and a few other short few words) is 14.

The (KDP) ISBN of this book is: ISBN: 9798390632703

I hope to publish some more Quechuan etymological links, including with Basque in an article on omniglot in the near future. I discovered these after writing this book, and before making these final edits. These new etymological links are not included in this book, but will be on the omniglot article, although a few of the Basque links I have already found in the past are included in this book. The main body of etymological connections in this book contains 53 'word points', these are not individual words, but 53 specific paragraphs or sections, each discussing a specific and different group of potentially related words. There are additional word origin comments and words discussed in the Chimakuan section and in the main body of text. Much of this book also discusses deep philosophy about language, philosophy, metaphysics and ancient history, as indicated in the title of this book.
I have also published a new book specifically on giants in the Old North and in North Wales, which also contains a little information about language links, and which further discusses some of the elements of giant lore discussed in this book (ISBN: 9798390632703). A reference to the Tylwyth Teg language is included in both books, although differently, and the other information in the two books is sometimes related, but discusses very different aspects of the topics in question, but the book published on the 14th of April being specifically about giants in the Old North and in North Wales, and completely different to the Native American languages discussed in this book (ISBN: 9798390632703) Although I technically published this book on giants in the Old North and North Wales on the 14th of April, and after I published this book with ISBN 9798390632703 on the 8th of April, I have since added some final edits to this book published on the 8th of April (ISBN: 9798390632703) hence why I refer to the book published on the 14th of April in the past tense. Both of these books and my other books are necessary for understanding all of my research on these topics. The newer book published on the 14th of April is titled *Prehistoric giants of The Old North/Yr Hen Ogledd and North Wales, with further comments on the ancient archaeology, mythology and prehistoric language of the Old North and North Wales*, ISBN: 9798387991950.

Contents:

Photo above: Signal Hill, a Hohokam archaeological site in southern Arizona. Although Hohokam culture was not connected to cultures in ancient Britain, the spiral designs on some of these rocks are very similar to some of those found in Britain, North Africa, and the Canary Islands. The spirals appear to have a form of inherent geometry, and although their exact meaning is unknown, I personally think that the abundance of these designs is connected to an ancient, worldwide knowledge of sound and of sacred geometry, a subject that this book explores. I also once included this photo in a different ebook in the past.

Introduction and underlying philosophy

For a long time it was the norm in post-industrial academic circles to assume a recent origin for the indigenous American languages. Thankfully anthropology, archaeology and science in general are slowly catching up to what the indigenous peoples say themselves, namely that they have been in the Americas since time immemorial. I have a friend who is Hopi, and in his history, the Hopi people did not come from anywhere else outside of the Americas. This concept of indigenous American people originating in the Americas is also found throughout the histories of other indigenous American people.

Whilst the Eskimo-Aleut languages are found on both sides of the Bering Strait and whilst the Athabaskan, Eyak, Tlingit and Haida languages may have a connection to Yeniseian languages of Siberia, as suggested in the Dene-Yeniseian language hypothesis, an idea first mentioned by Alfredo Trombetti in 1923, neither of these connections does in my opinion prove that any of the indigenous American peoples originated in Northern Eurasia.

When I look at the diversity of languages throughout the world, I find it very difficult indeed to believe that all have a single origin, at least not through our current reality and modern understanding of human history.

To try and explain how these languages might be connected without the need for migration, I will refer back to something that my Hopi friend told me. Namely, that in Hopi history, the world we are in now was not the first.

This is a subject steeped in metaphor and symbolism, but which also has, as I understand it, a very literal meaning as well. According to Hopi history from what I was told , when we humans were in the world previous to this one, we had not yet manifested into bodies (i.e. the bodies that we have now) and instead had a more raw, soft and open form which granted us the abilty to discern each other's thoughts. However my friend also informed me that although there was little need for verbal communication at that time, languages such as the Hopi and Keres languages were for example already extant in the previous world.

Consequently if we include this idea of previous worlds and the existance of a more geometric, primorial language into our current understanding of linguistics, that is if we take the oral histories of indigenous people seriously, and as truth, which I think we really should, then this presents a whole other dimension to explore in examining the origins of language in the Americas, and throughout the world.

I will not go too much into the potential metaphysics and philosophy that surrounds this topic worldwide, rather I will merely mention it as an alternative explanation for the various similarites in form found across languages and postulate that these similarites might in fact be due to mechanisms that exist outside and beyond any notion of colonisation

As my Hopi friend suggested being able to discern each other's thoughts in a previous world, I have wondered if in some way we were all able to perceive the nature of things on a more vibrational level, with our written and spoken languages today being in a sense echoes or manifested forms of the vibrational nature that we were once more able to perceive; meaning in a sense that our languages today could be extensions of, or specific spectrums of, an original underlying vibrational and geometric reality

Using this idea as a foundational framework, a word like 'rock' could not only be onomatopoeic but could also be an extension of the unique spectrum of the rock's metaphysical, full nature. Furthermore, I have often wondered if, over time, our senses became more prone to 'collapsing' different aspects of the universe's vibrational expressions such that we eventually lost the ability to so easily discern the thoughts of others and came to rely more heavily upon spoken, and now written language.

However, given this past vibrational expression, I have wondered as well, if perhaps all life (including rocks and stars for instance, from an animistic point of view) in some way refracts or to some degree performs a form of 'wave-collapse' or 'wave-creation', allowing for its form to be perceived and for it to in turn perceive other life. Yet because humans do this in a different and more limited way, based solely on our biological senses, this has resulted in the original vibrational form of things becoming the articulated words in language as we understand words and language today.

Whilst I use the terms 'wave collapse' or 'refract' throughout this book, I should clarify that it is but one way to describe the process I am speaking about. I do not mean to imply by using coined terminology that vibration is the true nature of everything, as some spiritualists have asserted.

Whilst a vibrational nature to reality is obviously important in some way, that doesn't mean that the original nature of things can necessarily be thought of so mechanically. It is for this reason that I also make use of the term 'wave-creation', to refer to the possibility that refracting, or collapsing things from a wavelength form, is also what creates the vibrational form to begin with.
For more comments on how a process like this may be described as being a form of refraction, see page 25.

Having set the parameters of our discussion, if there was a more 'geometric' form of language in the previous world, a language perhaps based on the frequencies of sound and light as they naturally relate to the physical world, then any similarities found between unrelated languages could perhaps be explained as our modern languages containing 'echoes', or refracted forms of these original sacred sounds, music or languages.

I am not saying that I think *all* extra-sensory phenomena are 'geometric' language, or 'telepathic language' exactly. I think that in some cases there is an even deeper kind of self-knowledge and sense of 'knowing'. But I feel that by and large, these phenomena, whether perceived through the mind or the body, have to do with our ability to 'download' and refract waves of some kind, (a form of wave-collapse), and that sometimes these waves take the form of light and sound, albeit perhaps not in the normally perceivable spectrums.

As a means of example, one may notice that many of the words, which will be detailed in the next section, appear somewhat onomatopoeic. i.e., the word in some way is connected to the natural 'sounds' associated with its denotative meaning. Put another way, if we interpret this on a more metaphysical level, we could say that these ancient words actually correspond in some way to the frequency of the thing in question. This is I think the nature of the phrase **"fe, fi, fo, fum"** as said by the giant, in the story of Jack and the Beanstalk.

Many traditions around the world emphasize the importance of language, sound and music. And in some sense, at the deepest roots of our languages, the subject and the object are the same thing. There is a form of singing practiced by the Sápmi people known as the joik, and it is often said that when somebody joiks, they do not joik 'about' something, they joik 'the thing' in question. So if a person was to joik in relation to a mountain, the syllables they speak are not 'about' the mountain, they 'are' the mountain, thus the ideas of subject and object collapse. What I am trying to explain here is that throughout world mysticism and culture there is an important connection between language and spirituality, between the words and sounds themselves and creation.

In writing about this subject and giving reference to other cultural perspectives on the world, like Hopi, I should note that these are my own personal thoughts and interpretations and they do not necessarily correspond to how Hopi or other indigenous peoples in the Americas interpret their own culture. Only an Indigenous person has the right to do that. What I am doing is merely following my own lines thought with regards to language, in the hopes that I might be able to understand something more of its origins.

A list of possible word connections (including with lots of

Quechuan words) (contains 53 word points).

[1] The words on the 11 pages after this one (7 to 17), are included to demonstrate the possibility of existing links.The aforementioned Dene-Yeniseian and Eskimo-Aleut languages are not included here, except for one Tlingit word example. I have studied many languages to varying degrees and here I am really just trying to give an overview of some of the best examples of these possible connections, including some which I have only noticed recently. Most but not all of the word points on the following pages connect to Quechuan in some way. Many are also connected to Finnish. Many links to other languages are also included, indigenous American and many other languages. Each number in the list on the following pages is followed by a suggestion of possibly connected etymologies. I do not try to reconstruct the original sounds or meaning, so how I introduce each concept or 'word point' depends on the examples given. The numerals "one" and "two" are both discussed as one word point (see word point 14). This is because I feel that the roots for the two numbers may be related. Points about connections regarding forms of the numbers 3, 4, 5, 6 and 10 are discussed in points 15, 16, 17, 18 and 19 respectively. The numerical points focus mainly on Andean

---

1   *The wordlist introduced above and available from the following page to the end of page 17, is not exhaustive, and my other works include a large number of etymologies which in some cases connect to the words in this list but are not included here.*

languages and possible links with Uralic and other languages, but some non-Andean Indigenous American numbers are also briefly discussed. In addition to the etymologies themselves, something about the semantics and expanded possible meanings of these connections, such as their ancient meanings is discussed. The references are mostly in order, but not entirely, due to some later changes I made when writing this section. Words which are not given with references are those which I have already learned/know well enough to be certain of them.

I do not introduce all word points in the same way, in the first examples listed below and on the following pages, I say, "a word for…" and then as I continue, the way in which I discuss the word connections in the word points tend to be more specialised. After the words, there is a further section specifically on Chimakuan, followed by the other sections of this book.

1. - a word for 'fish'. Southern Quechua **challwa** – 'fish'. This word in more or less identical forms exists across many Quechuan and other languages from the same parts of the Andes, such as Aymara. I can see some possible similarity to Finnish **kala** – fish, for example, and some other examples from Uralic languages such as Northern Sámi **guolli** – fish. From what I understand **challwa** can be quite a generic word for 'fish', and considering the word's distribution this makes a lot of sense, I think. For example, Kichwa has another word **aychawa** (1) for 'fish' alongside **challwa**, and there are many others across the Quechuan languages. Other possible cognates of **challwa** may be Chatino Zacatepec **kula** – fish (2) and Ende (Papua New Guinea) **kollba** (3) – fish.

Compare also Proto-Afro-Asiatic: ***kall-** fish (4), most of the Afro-Asiatic cognates have a suffix, -m, but the original root according to (4) is ***kall-**.

2. - an interrogative suffix. Southern Quechua -**chu**, a suffix employed for negative sentences, but on its own it is an interrogative, e.g., ¿**rimankichu Qhichwa simita wasiyki?** - do you (singular) speak Quechua at home/in your house? Sometimes in Quechua the verb 'to be' is not used in Quechua, for example ¿**challwachu?** - a fish? Is it a fish? In Finnish it is possible to use the interrogative suffix -**ko** or -**kö** in a similar way. In certain Finnish sentences **kalako** would mean 'a fish?'. In Finnish this suffix is commonly seen on verbs, e.g., **tiedämme** – we know, versus **tiedämmekö?** - do we know? But in certain contexts, it can be attached to nouns, e.g.:
Person one: **se tanssi järvessä** (it dances in the lake)
Person two: **Mikä? Kalako?** (What? The fish?).

A Finnish friend helped me with understanding the usage of -**ko** with nouns. Another example mentioned to me by a friend is the interrogative particle **ka** in Japanese.

3. – a word for 'dog' and some other animals. This is a potential ancient root word which I first came across when trying to search for the etymology of Irish **sionnach** – fox. Little did I know that this Irish word could have potential cognates in indigenous American languages. For example, Chatino Zacatepec **šne?** – dog (2). A Proto-Afro-Asiatic root is reconstructed by Alexander Militarev and Olga Stolbova as ***wVŝin- ~ *wVnVŝ-** (4) meaning wolf, jackel, Egyptian **wnš** (4) - wolf, with some Berber languages having the ***wVŝin-** form, e.g., Semlal: **uššən** (4). This word bares similarities to a number of words for similar animals around the world besides the Chatino Zacatepec, possibly Irish **sionnach** – fox, for example, Lakota **šúŋka** – dog, Tehuelche **'wačn** – dog (5), Selk'nam **wisn?** (6) - dog, and **wàhṣ** (6) - fox. Perhaps more distantly to Yaghan **yašala** – dog (7). Other possible indigenous South American cognates include Lengua **simhiŋ** – dog (8) and De'kwana **sɨ?na** - dog (9), Proto-Arawakan ***tsinu** – dog, jaguar (10) perhaps Imbabura Kichwa **añas** – fox (11), and perhaps Kichwa **siniq** – fox (1), although this word is marked as *neo.* in source 1. Note that the Selk'nam word **wàhṣ** may show the initial syllable represented in Proto-Afro-Asiatic ***wVŝin-** (4), also visible in Tsimshian **haas** – dog (12), Nuxalk has **wats'** – dog, whereas most of the other examples relate more closely to the **ŝin-** part of the Proto-Afro-Asiatic etymology. The Imbabura Kichwa word **añas** (11) perhaps shows more similarity to the Egyptian **wnš** (4). There are also other possible cognates, not included here.

4. – another word for 'dog'. I have seen some similarities between Finnish **koira** – dog, Hausa **kare** – dog, Qawesqar **ḳyoro** - dog (13), Proto-Cariban ***akôrô** – dog (14), to give some examples.

5. – a word connected to sacred power and spirit. Kichwa **waka** – sacred (adjective), temple (noun) (1), also in other Quechuan languages, a word which has at least in some Quechuan languages been named with pyramid sites in Peru, in the Quechuan forms of their names, e.g. **Wak'a Pukllana**, a Wari pyramid in Lima, hispanicised as *Huaca Pucllana.* From what I understand, **wak'a** is a word connected to sacred sites and to the power or spirit connected with those sites. I am not a good speaker of Quechua and I think only a native speaker of that language could really convey this word's exact meaning. To me, however, this word bares a similarity to the Finnish word **väki**. In modern Finnish this may translate to something like a 'crowd' of people or 'force' of people, but originally it meant something like 'power', 'force', 'spirit' connected with a particular natural locale . In Finnish spirituality for example, a lake, a forest or a mountain had their own **väki** which had to be respected and treated with care. Although the Finnish and Quechuan meanings are without doubt different, in my opinion, the general meaning conveyed is very similar. The Lakota word **wakȟáŋ** is another example of a word that I cannot explain or try to translate into English. But from what I understand it also refers to a kind of 'power' or 'force'.

6. - a word for 'copper'. The word **anta** means 'copper' in some Quechuan languages, and the indigenous peoples of the Andes had great skill in working with this metal. I think that the word shows some similarity to Egyptian **ḥmt, hmt, hmty** – 'bronze' or 'copper', and Old Irish **umae** – copper, bronze, Irish **umha**, Welsh **efydd**. Both Ireland and Wales also have prehistoric Bronze Age copper mines, such as those at Ross Island near Killarney in Ireland, and those at Y Gogarth and Parys in Wales.

7. – a word connected to the sun. Chatino Zacatepec **kʷičā** - sun (2), compare for example Finnish **kesä** – summer, Erzya **кизэ** (kize) - summer or year. Other possible cognates in the Americas include Proto-Muskogean **xasiCi** (15) – 'sun', Proto-Algonquian ***ki·še?Өwa** (16) – sun and Beothuk **keeose** (17) – sun or moon.

8. - A word for 'pine tree' or 'tree': Chatino Zacatepec **yka kitʸē** - pine (2), the noun element **kitʸē** shows some resemblence to Finnish **kuusi** – pine, Scottish Gaelic **giuthas** – a Scots pine tree, and perhaps more distantly to the ***kVt-** like root seen in Welsh **coed** – forest, for instance, 'Cumbric' ***ke:t-**, Cornish **coos**, Breton **koad**. From my own research there are several examples of similar words from non-Indo-European languages, for example Proto-Nilotic ***kɛ-ɛt** or ***kɪ-yat** – tree (18) and Tamil **kātu** - a forest.

9. – a word connected to boats and water; perhaps visible in Kichwa **wanpu** – boat, ship (1), and **wambu** – canoe (1) and **wampuna** – to float, to raft, to swim (1). The initial consonant and the nasal make this word similar to Finnish and Estonian **vene** – boat, in my opinion. In reference (46) (an article I wrote on omniglot) I mention some other examples of this potential word cognate, which I noticed previously, including Selk'nam **yèni** (6) – canoe. In this new book I am adding the Quechua words. Some other potential links I came across recently are Proto-Arawakan ***wene** – water (19), and Waorani **wi-po** – canoe (20). I do not think that this group of words collectively come from a word for 'boat', I think it more likely that their original sacred meaning was pertained to types of movement connected to water, whether that be a boat on the water or the water itself.

10. – the words llama and lamb. Southern Quechua **llama** – a llama, bares some similarity to Finnish **lammas** – sheep, and English 'lamb' and forms in related languages. The word **llama** is also applied to lambs in the Kichwa language.

11. - A word for 'sand'. I think perhaps that the Finnish word **hiekka** – sand, could have some related words in indigenous South American languages, including, Proto-Carib ***saka(w)** – sand (14) and Gününa Küne **cʔixɨy** – sand (21), Upper Chehalis **cʔa'χæ?s** - sand (22).

12. - A word for 'mountain'. In a different previous omniglot article (reference 47) I talked a little about a possible similarity between the Italic and some Celtic words for 'mountain' and a few words for mountain in indigenous American languages. These words are I think based on a root, roughly reconstructable as *men-, for example English 'mountain', French **montagne**, Spanish **montaña**, Welsh **mynydd**, Scottish Gaelic **monadh** to give some examples. There is also a Basque word, **mendi** for 'mountain'. As well as the Squamish and Hawaiian words for 'mountain', there are I think further related words, especially in the Salishan languages, e.g. Halkomelem **smeent** – mountain, Nuxalk **smnt** or **smt** – mountain, Sqamish **smánit**. Other possible connected words include Upper Chehalis language there is the word **'maniči-mountain** (22), whilst a Proto-Mazatec reconstructed word for 'hill' is ***nįˀntúˀ** (23), to give some examples.

13. A word for 'mountain' and 'earth'. In Finnish there is a word, **mäki**, which means a 'hill' essentially, Estonian **mägi**, also Khanty **мӯг**. More specifically, wiktionary defines the meaning of the Finnish word as "a relatively large, usually rounded elevation of earth; generally larger than *kukkula* ("hill, hillock") and smaller than *vuori* ("mountain") (Wiktionary). In some ways I think the word **mäki** is also connected to the shape of the earth, rather than necessarily to what might be defined as a mountain generally. It might be possible that certain indigenous American languages contain similar words with meanings of 'mountain' or 'earth', for example Upper Chehalis **'məkʷˀ-** (22) - mountain or hill, which exists in addition to that word for 'mountain' discussed in point 12. Another possible example of a meaning similar to 'earth' is the Lakota word **makhá** – earth, soil. Another couple of related words may exist in the Pacaas Novos language, **makan?** - earth, land (24), and **pakun** - mountain, hill, stone (24); and others, such as Catquina **maši** - mountain, hill (25), Ese Ejja (Huarayo) **meši** - earth, ground, soil, land, world (26), and perhaps Quechuan (many languages) **pacha** – earth, ground, world, universe. Another couple of examples are Mosetén **mœˈkæ** (27) - mountain or hill, and Mashco Piro **mahka** (28) - mountain or hill, which bare a closer resemblance to the Uralic forms.

14. – the numbers 'one' and 'two' in Finnish are **yksi** and **kaksi**. Whilst I think it is difficult to determine the origin of these numbers, they essentially seem to duplicate the consonants [k] and [s]; in the Northern Sámi language, the numbers 'one' and 'two' are **okta** and **guokte**. These numbers also show a similar duplication, but of [k] and [s]. The Kichwa numbers for 'one' and 'two' show what is arguably a similar duplication, 'one' is **shuk** and 'two' is **ishkay**. My Hopi friend told me that in his language the number 'one' is **sùukya'** and this is its *counting form*, it comes from the word **suu-** one, and -**kya'**- a nominalising suffix. If the Hopi numbers are somehow connected to the others given in this paragraph, then perhaps the Hopi language tells us a new level of meaning to how these numbers are formed, if indeed they are

connected in some way. Comments on the Hopi number 4 are below on this page.

(Further note: the Chumashan numbers for 'one' and 'two' are **pakaš** (45) and **'iškom̓** (45) both of which show a form of [s] and [k] in these numerals.

15. The number 'three' in Finnish is **kolme**, and **golbma** in Northern Sámi. The Kichwa word is **kimsa**, and the Aymara it is also **kimsa**. On their own these look less likely to be related to the Uralic number 'three' due to their being no [l] in the Quechuan and Aymara word, although the Mapuche word for 'three' is **küla** which does show an [l]. In this example the Uralic word may help to make sense of how the Quechuan, Aymaran and Mapuche words are connected.

16. Finnish **neljä** – four, also bares some similarity to Mapuche **meli** – four. Hopi **naalöyö'** - four, is similiar, and is based on the number two, which is **lööyö'** in the counting form. If again the Hopi number is connected to the others, then the Hopi number preserves further levels of meaning through the fact that the original, separate components of these words have individual grammaticalised meaning.

17. Kichwa **pichka** – five, and Aymara **pheska** – five, arguably show some similarity to Finnish **viisi** – five, and Northern Sámi **vihtta** – five, if the [ʊ] in Finnish, Sámi [v] is equivalent to the variant of [p] in Kichwa and Aymara. Another word of similar appearance is the Basque – **bost** – five, which also means 'fist' in the Basque language, providing perhaps another layer of meaning. The Turkic numbers for 'five' also show some similarity, e.g. Altai **беш** /beš/.

18. Kichwa **sukta** and Aymara **sojjta** – six, bare some similarity to Indo-European terms for 'six'.

19. Kichwa **chunka** – ten, may bare a similarity to Finnish **kymmenen** – ten, and to Basque **hamar** – ten. Another similarity may be seen in Aymara **tunca** – ten, compare English 'ten'.

20. A word for 'snake' or a mythical snake, Guaraní **mbói** – a kind of snake, shows some similarity to Abinomn **moi** – water snake (29). Abinomn is a likely language isolate spoken in the Papua province of Indonesia. This word is quite different to the other cognates I have proposed, and I have noticed for instance that to some degree Tupian and Macro-Gê languages have a lot of vocabulary which, as of yet, I have not seen any equivalent to in other languages. This is why I included this word specifically because it may show a relationship between southeast Asian and certain indigenous American

languages east of the Andes. Possibly connected to Proto-Afro-Asiatic: ***biʔVy-** snake (4), Egyptian **byȝ** – holy serpent (4).

21. Quechua **ñan** – path, way (in many Quechuan languages), possibly connected to Tocharian B **nauntai** – road (35), possibly also related to Tibetan **lam** – path, and to Welsh **nant** – valley. The word 'Nanny' in Northern English placenames may be related to the Welsh **nant**, but here at least in one place the meaning seems connected to ancient sites that are in a straight line, so, it may be quite different to the Welsh meaning. The Welsh meaning of 'valley', also Cornish **nans** – valley, may specifically imply a meaning connected to that of a valley of water, specifically. The Brythonic words also contain this -t suffix, which is not found in the Northern English placenames. There are I think other connections with this word, but the etymologies seem to become very much related to water and movement.

Perhaps also related to Kichwa **nuna** (1) – soul, and Ancient Egyptian **nnw** – primordial waters.

22. – Kichwa **killa** – moon (1), possibly related to Tibetan **zla** (zla ba) – moon. Compare also Udmurt **толэзь** /toleź/ - moon, also Eastern Mari **тылзе** /tylze/ - moon.

23. – A root word connected to 'light'. Finnish **valo** – light may be seen as similar to Kichwa **p'allala** (1) – 'light', an example of where Finnish [ʋ] may be equivalent to a variant of [p]. I am not sure whether or not the spelling **p'** in Quechua represents an ejective form of [p], ejective consonants exist in some Quechuan languages certainly.

24. – A root word for 'water, pool' which may be related to the root word 23 above through the sense that both water and light move in waves. Finnish **valo** – light, bares some similarity to **Vellamo**, the name of a Finnish sea goddess. If we replace [ʋ] with a variant of [p] or [b], similarities to words connected to water may become more obvious. For example, the Welsh word **pwll** – pool, Scottish Gaelic **poll** – mud, pool, area that floods (particularly in placenames), Irish **poll** – mud, etc. The word **poll** is found in Northern Norwegian placenames, for example, in the Lofoten islands, where it refers to a 'pool' or 'lake' of seawater, essentially a lake connected to the sea, which is saline due to the 'pooling' of tidal water into the lake. There is also Proto-Basque: ***balśa** - pool, pond (30) (with various other meanings). In terms of indigenous American languages, there may be a similarity in Kal'ina **palana** – the ocean (31), Kal'ina **pilipili** – the swamp (31), also Q'eqchi' Mayan **palaw** – sea (32). Also Proto-Afro-Asiatic ***bVl(Vl)-** (4) flow, overflow and Proto-Afro-Asiatic ***bVlVg- / *bVlVḳ-** (4) 'shine', the latter of which leads back to this possible connection between water and light. There are also many so-called Indo-European cognates which I would argue testify to the relationship

between the meanings of 'water' and 'light', particularly in my opinion, with regards to the movement of light and water in a particular way. Another possible example that refers to water in the sky, aka cloud, is Proto-Nilotic *pɔɔl (18) – cloud.

One may see further connections here to words like 'well' and 'swell' in English, Proto-Salishan *swVl- or *wVl- (see reference 48 for an article with some more on this). Furthermore, the formula *sVl- may imply a meaning connected to 'light' as well as to water, for example Irish **solas** – light, Irish **súil** – eye, Finnish **silmä** – eye, etc; perhaps in the sense of light 'flowing into' the eye. Compare also Aymara **sulʸa** – dew (40).

25. the word **t'inka** is an indigenous Andean word, which from what I understand is a kind of honorary word, a way of acknowledging the ancestors and gods, although I do not precisely understand the meaning. I think that it shows some similarity to Indo-European words for 'think', with Proto-Tocharian: ***täṅkwä** (33) meaning 'love'. Compare also English 'thank', German **danke** etc, although the Tocharian meaning is I think very important in this context.

It may be that the word **t'inka** is associated with a 'first offering' to the goddess **Pachamama** 'earth/universe mother'.

26. In Finnish, **sumu** means 'fog', which is rather like the Kichwa **samay** which means 'soul' (1). I believe that any connection between these words is 'metaphysical', and the connection between the sacred, and 'water', can also be seen in the etymology of the Latin word DEVS – 'god', which is related to the English word 'dew'. Note also Kichwa **sami** (1) – breath or courage, and in other Quechuan languages **samay** can mean 'breath' showing a possibly clear association with cloud or water vapour.

27. Quechuan **simi** – mouth, word, language, appears somewhat similar to Finnish **sana** – word.

28. Kichwa **k'allu** – tongue (1), other Quechuan **qallu** – tongue, language, shows some similarity to Finnish **kieli** – language. Similar interrelationships might be seen across multiple language families, for example Mongolian **xol** – language, **til** means 'language' in many Turkic languages, also likely related to Mongolian **хэл** (xel) - tongue, language.

29. Quechuan **noqa, ñuqa** – first person singular pronoun (I), is very close to a variety of other words for this pronoun in different languages, including Haisla (a Wakashan language) **-nugʷ(a)** (37), Tocharian A **ɲuk** (34) – 'I', the feminine first-person singular pronoun, Ancient Egyptian ⌒𓎡 **ink** – first

person singular pronoun, independent, non-attached. Sometimes ⌐ᴁ is vocalised as **nuk**.

30. Quechuan (many languages) **kaspi** – stick, compare Finnish **kasvi** – plant, vegetable, related to **kasvaa** – to grow. Another example of Finnish [ʋ] being equivalent to [p]? Also Kichwa **kaspa** (1) -' any of various edible seeds' (1). Compare also Basque **hazia** – seed, Kallawaya **kies** – seed (38). Compare also Tlingit **ḵáas'** – stick. Compare also Komi **көйдыс** /köjdys/ - seed.

Above is the only Kallawaya word included in this book. My previous work regarding Kallawaya is available in the ebooks section of my bookofdunbarra website, the article in the eBook is titled *The language of ancient navigators and the Puquina/Paracas people, and other language links between Europe and pre- Columbian America* and was originally written under a pseudonym. It is on pages 140, 141, 142, 143, 144, 145, 146, 147, 148, 149, 150, 151, 152, 153 in the eBook *Ancient languages and their connections, second edition, The Land of Pink Sky.* [2]

31. Quechuan (many languages) **qara** - bark of a tree or skin, compare Finnish **kuori** - skin, bark, husk, shell.

32. Quechuan (many languages) **tullu** – bone, compare Finnish **luuta** – bone, with consonant reversal taken into account; formulaic base: L-U-T or T-U-L or T-L + U (reduplicated?).

33. Quechuan **urqu** – mountain, perhaps connected to English 'rock', Breton **roc'h** and through extension and by consonant re-arrangement to words meaning 'rock' or 'mountain' similar to the formula *kVr-.

33. Kichwa **q'iwina** (1) – to twist, perhaps connected to Finnish **kääntää** – to turn, also Finnish **keinuttaa** – to rock, from **keinua** – to swing, rock, roll, compare Scottish Gaelic **tionndaidh** – turning.

34. Kichwa **yura** – tree (1), perhaps connected to Finnish **juuri** – root, as in, root of a tree.

35. Possibly similar to the meaning of **wak'a/waka**, Kichwa **waq-** is a root connected to 'voice', e.g., **waqana** (1) – call out, compare Indo-European roots based upon the approximate sounds *wek- or *wak- which gives 'voice' through the Latin, also for example Tocharian A **wak** (34) – 'voice'.

36. Quechuan (several languages) **wasi** – house, bares some similarity to Tocharian A **waṣt** – house (34).

---

2   *This eBook is available on this page: https://www.bookofdunbarra.co.uk/16-ebooks*

37. Kichwa **manya** – beach, border (1), possibly Tocharian B **manarko** – beach (35). I think that the Kichwa word could possibly be connected to Kichwa **man** – towards (1) and -**manta** (from, out of) in some other Quechuan languages; with the word for 'beach' being connected in the sense of 'heading away from' (or towards?) the land or sea. Another possible related word is Guanche **manse** – shore (36).

38. Quechuan (several languages), **piqchu** – mountain, pyramidal-shaped rock, possibly connected to Q'eqchi' Mayan **pek** – stone, compare also Old Norse **pík** – mountain, peak, English 'peak', or 'pike' in Northern English place-names. Although there is an Indo-European etymology for 'peak', the Semantic meaning in Norse and in Northern English placenames can refer more specifically to a mountain, again sometimes with a pyramidal appearance. Possibly Proto-Afro-Asiatic ***mik-** 'stone' (4).

39. Quechuan **qucha** – lake, several languages, likely connected to Aymara **quta** – lake, possibly connected to Proto-Afro-Asiatic ***gad-** riverbed (4). In order to further demonstrate this, I need to find other possible cognates. I have noticed possible cognates to the Proto-Afro-Asiatic term in European languages, but not thus far in the Americas (that I can remember).

40. Quechuan (several languages) **wayra** – wind, possibly connected to Proto-Afro-Asiatic ***rVwun-** 'wind' (4). Compare also Ainu **réra** – wind.

41. Quechuan (several languages) **inti** – sun, compare Proto-Afro-Asiatic ***yatin-/*ʔetin-** 'sun' (4), Egyptian **itn** – sun. Note that in Ancient Egypt, different names were given to the sun depending on the position it took in the sky, from what I understand. Furthermore, some traditions state that there have been several 'suns' shining on earth throughout human history, so words for 'sun' may not have originally referred to the sun that we see today.

42. Proto-Chibchan ***hak ~ *kaʔ** – stone (39), perhaps connected to Proto-Afro-Asiatic ***ḥak-** stone (4).

43. Quechuan **k'ullu** – wood, perhaps connected distantly to Scottish Gaelic **coille** – forest, also found in Irish as **coill** and in Old Irish as **caill** – wood, forest.

44. Quechuan **kallpa** – strength, force, power, energy, strong, perhaps connected to the **cal-** prefix found in Celtic languages which means 'hard, strong' e.g., Welsh **caled** – strong, also perhaps found in Latin in the word **calx** – limestone, possibly related to Greek **χάλιξ** /khálix/ - pebble. It appears that the forms in Indo-European languages are of a more ancient origin and not specifically Indo-European. Also compare Quechua **khallki** - cobblestone, paving-stone.

45. Quechuan **khumara** - sweet potato, likely connected to Maori **kūmara** - a sweet potato. (I noticed this connection mentioned on Wiktionary and that is how I learned of it). This example pretty demonstratively proves that the indigenous people of the Andes were connected with the Polynesians or their ancestors in some way.

46. Quechuan **manqu** – base, foundation, ferret, perhaps connected to the *men- root in Indo-European languages when implying the meaning of 'mountain' and 'go up' and 'go out', perhaps through extension connected to Welsh **maen** – stone, Cornish **mên** – stone, and to word 37 of this list.

47. Quechuan **saruy** – a track, perhaps linked to Proto-Afro-Asiatic *čVr(a) - a furrow (4) and to Welsh **seri** – a footpath or causeway.

48. Quechuan **sinqa** – nose, the first two consonants are similar to the *sn- in English 'sneeze', 'snore', 'sniff', which are all related to noses in some way. Proto-Afro-Asiatic also has ***sVn-** 'to smell'.

49. Quechuan **p'uti** – chubby, compare English 'fat', Danish **fed**, Norwegian **feit**, The forms in Sámi languages such as Northern Sámi **buoide** – fat, show more similarity to the Quechuan word. Like in the case of many Sámi words, Wiktionary gives the etymology of the Sámi words as coming from the Germanic, when in fact there is no actual proof that this is the case, and the assumption that several words in Sámi languages come from Germanic languages is I think often an unfounded assumption. Rather than these Sámi words being of Germanic origin, I think that mostly they are from ancestral languages which simultaneously gave rise to a set of vocabulary in Sámi and in Germanic.

50. Quechuan **panti** - dark red or reddish violet, compare Finnish **punainen** – red, from **puna** – red, possibly also related to Erzya **пона** /pona/ which means 'hair'.

51. Quechuan **qalla** – wheel, spindle, round stone, perhaps connected to Indo-European *kel- whence comes the English word 'wheel'. Often it seems assumed that the wheel is somehow connected to the emergence of Indo-European languages. However, the fact that Indo-European languages commonly have a word for a circular, wheel-like shape or wheel, is not proof that Indo-European languages are specifically connected to the wheel. There are many circular, wheel-shaped things in nature, but furthermore, if the Indo-European word for 'wheel' is connected to the Quechuan word for wheel-like device or round shape, it further demonstrates that this idea that Indo-European languages brought the wheel may well be false.

This list with two more word points and explanation continues for another page after this.

52. Aymara **urpu** – fog (40), this word appears similar to an Indo-European root for 'sky', e.g. Welsh **wybr** – sky, and for example Tocharian A **eprer-** - sky (34).

53. Quechuan **ranki** – dawn, possibly connected to Finnish **aurinko** – sun. If so, the word is probably also connected to Finnish **auer** – haze, and possibly to Latin **aurora** – sky. These word links are however problematic, as some forms show a medial d or so, for example older Finnish **auder**, and Lithuanian **aušra** – dawn, Russian **ýтро** /utro/ - morning, and English 'east', Norwegian **aust** etc. If the words are connected, then perhaps the intermediate consonant before -r is part of a separate prefix, not visible in the Quechuan, Finnish and Latin word forms. If the Quechuan and Finnish forms are based upon a form like *(V)(u)rank(V), then the Proto-Dravidian ***nē-r-** - time, sun (41) and ***ńēsir-** (?) - sun (41) show how a similar group of three consonants are behaving, in this case the form ***nē-r-** contains consonants which correspond to the *(V)(u)rank(V) form, but the consonants are in reverse, whereas the forms like **aušra** may correspond more to the form ***ńēsir-** (?).

I think that the form *(V)(u)rank(V) could also be connected to Ancient Greek **oὐρᾱ́** /ourā́/ - 'tail'. Although this link is distant, I think that at a basic level the sound *ora or *oro is connected to the colour gold, to circular movement, power, energy and to sunlight. Although **oὐρᾱ́** is connected to a word for 'buttocks', the **oὐρᾱ́** as in **oὐροβόρος**, ouroboros, is a symbol I think deeply connected with the sun and to the type of energy produced by the sun. I cannot yet explain how the 'tail' concept fits in, but if we take the meaning more closely to be 'buttocks', then symbolically these are connected to a round shape and to the idea of eating one's own excrement in the form of that shape. Even though this is not a particularly fun topic, I think it kind of necessary to explain how words for 'buttocks' might be connected to eternity and to our relationship with the sun. In the mythology of many cultures the soul energy that we have is connected with that of the sun, and this idea of back-and-forth movement, just as we consume sunlight and life is possible through sunlight.
By extension, excrement is somewhat of a golden colour, like the sun, hence Indo-European words for 'gold' based upon the root *or-, and this alchemical idea that urine could be used to create gold and give eternal life et cetera. Not only is gold also created by the sun, but this idea of 'gold' being somewhat that was once consumed, broken down and 'eaten' by the sun from other forms of matter, is kind of crucial I think to this symbolism.

In a fictional sense, the German writer Michael Ende also refers to a magical ouroboros-shaped object as the **Auryn**.

Possible connections between the Chimakuan, Celtic and Afro-Asiatic languages

Written by Linden Alexander Pentecost on January 2nd 2023.

Photo above: Tamanowas Rock, *This file is licensed under the Creative Commons Attribution-Share Alike 3.0 Unported license*, photo by Jon Roanhaus. A link to the licence is here: https://creativecommons.org/licenses/by-sa/3.0/deed.en – I made some edits to the colour and sharpness of the original photo, as well as cropping it slightly. The original is available here: https://commons.m.wikimedia.org/wiki/Category:Tamanowas_Rock#/media/File%3ATamanowas_Rock_NRHP_15000498_Jefferson_County%2C_WA.jpg

Tamanowas rock is a sacred site to several indigenous peoples on the Olympic Peninsula, including the Chimakuan-speaking peoples, who have known and gone to this site for at least ten thousand years. This sacred site may even have been a tsunami-refuge area. I mention this site because I feel that it helps to tie together the incredibly ancient presence of the Chimakuan languages and peoples within this landscape and their sacred connection to it.

Below and on the following page I discuss some Proto-Chimakuan words and their possible relationship to words in other languages. Again, this is not meant in any way to imply that these words came from Europe or Africa, but rather I use these words to demonstrate that these languages as a whole perhaps have deep, ancient connections with one another, although these connections may be relatively small when compared to the vast amounts of vocabulary in the Americas that have no equivalent elsewhere.

In much the same way as the preceding word list, the following discusses possible etymological connections of the Chimakuan languages to the Indo-European and Afro-Asiatic languages. Chimakuan languages are an ancient family of languages from the Olympic Peninsula in Washington State and I dedicate this work to the Quileute and Makah indigenous peoples.

The Proto-Chimakuan words given below and on the following page are from *Powell, James V. 1974. Proto-Chimakuan: Materials for a Reconstruction. Ph.D. dissertation. Honolulu: University of Hawaii.*

*-kina – to say or tell, perhaps distantly connected to Irish *can* – to sing, Welsh *canu* – to sing, Ancient Greek καναχέω kanakhéō and with many other examples across Indo-European, Proto-Afro-Asiatic *kVnVy- - say, call (1), Egyptian kny – call (1), Western Chadic *kwa/un- 'say' or 'tell' (1), possibly Lithuanian kanklės – a type of instrument, and the related Finnish word kantele, referring to an ancient string instrument

*kináno – dog, similar to English 'canine', English 'hound', from Proto-Indo-European *k(w)V – dog, which is *k(w)Vn- in some genitive and nominative forms. Compare also Canarian (Guanche) cuna – dog (1), Western Chadic *kwin-H- (1), Proto-Afro-Asiatic *kwVHen- (1), Proto-Sino-Tibetan: *qhʷīj (2), *qhʷīn (2) and others.

*lakʷi- - to lick. This word shows some clear similarity to the English word 'lick', which is attested across Indo-European, and may be reconstructed as *leig- or *liig-. also Proto-Afro-Asiatic *lVḳ- 'lick' (1), with other possible examples in other language families

*laqʷa- slimy, possibly related to the word above, and to various other examples of similar forms across world languages.

*loq̓ʷa- - hole, cave or tunnel, possibly related to Proto-Chumash *loq – hole (3), Proto-Mayan *luqum – earthworm (4), Proto-Muskogean *olakkʷi – hole

(5), Aymara **laq'u** - worm, English 'lug' as in dialectal 'lugs' – ears, and 'lugworm'. Although 'lug' is usually interpreted as meaning 'slow' I think that with regards to the words lugworm and lugs – ears, the meaning may be 'hole' rather than 'slow'.

*laẏ- - near, towards, perhaps connected to Welsh lle – a place, the Finnish -lla/-llä suffix meaning approximately 'in' 'by' or 'at', Finnish lähellä – near, from lähi- near or close.

*ɬaq̇ʷo (?) - eye, perhaps related to Welsh llygad – eye, Cornish lagaz – eye, Sanskrit locona – eye. This word I think is one of the most convincing pieces of evidence in my opinion for a specific connection between Chimakuan and Celtic.

*ƛap- - bed, Proto-Afro-Asiatic *lab- (1) - side of body

*ṁas- - to lift, heavy, related perhaps to English 'mass'

*paɬ- - flat, perhaps connected to Indo-European *plet-, German platt, English 'flat' etc

*pil- - mouth, speak, perhaps related to Irish béal – mouth

*ṗiƛa- (ṗiƛa- ?) - to fill, full, perhaps connected to English 'pool', Welsh pwll, Scottish Gaelic and Irish poll, Norwegian dialectal poll, all meaning roughly a pool or area that fills with water. Perhaps also connected to word point 24 given earlier in this book, on page 12 of this book.

Comments on elongated skulls and pyramids in relation to language

Several cultures around the world, including some in the Americas, practiced a form of artificial cranial deformation to produce an elogated or cone-shaped skull. There are multiple reasons for this practice, but anthoropologists often take the view that it had to do with social status. I personally am more inclined to think that this pratice had more to do with spiritual status within a community, at least originally. I think that this is also perhaps visible in the typical depictions of witches and wizards that one encounters in Europe, i.e. cone-shaped   hats.

While I do not believe that Sumeria was the origin of civilisation, nor that their history is more relevent and correct than that of other cultures, in ancient

Sumeria, there were a group of deities called **Apkallu** that appear to have come from the sea, to teach a certain knowledge and were sometimes depicted as having what appears to be a fish superimposed onto their head, making the cranium appear more elongated. This may be an additional example of where spiritual status was symbolised and expressed through the wearing of a conical shaped headdress. However, turning to the fish/sea element in **Apkallu** symbolism, perhaps this association is due to the fact that water refracts light, in much the same way a prism does.

As mentioned in another Omniglot article (see reference 46) cephalopods have an ability to communicate via light and the shape of a squid, cuttlefish or octopus' head, is arguably similar in shape to that of an elongated human head. Pyramids exhibit a different but arguably similar shape, and just as prisms and water refract light, I feel that somehow, pyramids are symbolically connected to this. Yet, given the ability of cephalopods to communicate via light, this could perhaps explain the cultural desire of some to emulate this form through the practice of cranial deformation. If so, the elongated skull could represent the human ability to 'tap into' the original language/music of creation, and to refract it/collapse the wavelengths into spoken human language. In this same vein, pyramids could perhaps be seen as a representation of this same process on a much larger scale.

Although I am not able to conclusively define the connections between these things, I do feel that mollusks, another aquatic life form, by virtue of their similar shape and geometry also play a very important role in this symbolism, hence why ancient shell middens, were often viewed as sacred sites. While there are many aspects to this symbolism, I would argue that this concept, of a spiral, forming a cone shape, a force of life emanating through water, is not only symbolically connected to the emergence of sound and light waves, but is also somehow connected to the very emergence of life itself.

On a further note, it is interesting I think that the Finnish word *vene* may show cognates in indigenous American languages, not because of any reference to boats or ancient sea travel, but rather because of a shared connection to the importance of water.

There are instances of gods or deities moving across water by boat, for example, **Väinämöinen** in Finnish history, and **Manannán Mac Lir** in Irish history. Both of these gods are incredibly important, but also equally mysterious in their respective cultures. I would argue that in some senses, the names **Väinämöinen** and **Manannán** bare a certain similarity, although the etymology of both is not satisfactorily concluded.

My personal view is that these possible connections have little to do with an ancient seafaring culture, but instead have to do with this concept of life and wisdom eminating through water. Even though some of these concepts between cultures are more similar than others, this basic idea, connected to life and to water is to my knowledge, found in every culture I have studied. That being said, I do not believe that there was ever a single world civilisation, or a civilisation more advanced than others. Furthermore, I do not believe for instance that the Egyptians taught the Inca and their ancestors how to build pyramids; the pyramids of Perú being entirely indigenous innovations.

However, in a previous world, before we became humans, in a previous reality, the mathematics and 'pre-language' of the ancestors of the people who eventually became the Egyptians and the Incas, *may* have perhaps been connected. In other words, a similar knowledge of original "sounds" and structural bases may have been present in both cultures, but I think that these things were developed independently by their respective cultures through a physical medium, or a medium in this reality.

Comments on ancestors in relation to the previous topics, including giants

Although the topic of 'ancient giants and other ancestors' may seem out of place in this article, as this phenomena may not necessarily have much to do with similarities in language, it does have to do with the aforementioned discussion of previous worlds and/or earlier stages of humanoid development.

World history is replete with references to ancestors who are described as either much taller, or much shorter than us. Yet generally speaking "giants" and "small people" are often associated with and suggest earlier, more primordial times and places in mythology, at least as far as Britain and Ireland are concerned and do seem in some way, to bridge the gap between the physical and the mythological. Thus, they are I think a connection to an ancient other world in a sense. While within this whole topic we can also talk about gods in general, and other supernatural beings, which are perhaps all bridges between our world and the "otherworlds" or 'underworlds' that is beyond the scope of this work.

Fairy tales such as Jack the Giant Killer have formed our modern perception of giants as large dimwitted ogres that are sometimes said to eat humans. Yet, to what extent the appearance and characteristics of these beings can factually be applied to physical archaeology, is uncertain. Nevertheless, reports of supposed giant remains at places like Lovelock Cave in Nevada are not all together uncommon. But more importantly, 'giants' in mythology have symbolic meaning, with 'giants' often being connected to archetypal deities associated with nature, in European history at least; for example, the **jötnar** and **trolls** of Norse traditions, or the **Fomorians** in Goidelic traditions.

This seems to be the case with the **Saiduca/Si-Te-Cah** as mentioned in Paiute history that are described as having red hair and dwelling within the vicinity of the Lovelock Cave in Nevada. Due to the red hair, some seem to believe that reference to these giants suggests the possibility of European descent, but on the contrary, red hair appears throughout human history and in multiple parts of the world, so if the red hair does have a more physical as well as symbolic meaning, it is not a meaning that can definitively nor exclusively suggest a connection to modern Europeans in my opinion. Furthermore, not all mentions of giants within Indigenous American history describe them as having red hair.

Regarding the Giants of Lovelock Cave, there is evidence that in the past, the landscape was much wetter and that the nearby Humboldt Basin used to be a lake in ancient times. From this, something I found particularly interesting in the Paiute accounts is the belief that these beings are said to live in caves, and I wonder if this practice of living in caves occurred after a particular change in climate, such as that which turned the Humboldt lake into a more or less dry basin.

From what my Hopi friend told me, this specific human-like giant phenomena is not something attested in Hopi history. However, Hopi history does carry the memory of a time when the surface of the world was darker and wetter, and I can't help but wonder if the red hair reported in some of these giant stories, might have to do with a time when sunlight was somehow different to what it is today, and that perhaps an event of sorts took place, causing the land to become drier, and the sunlight more harmful to these potentially early peoples, causing them to live in caves. I make mention of this fact as red-haired people are sometimes more prone to sunburn. Furthermore, in Shetlandic mythology, Picts/Pechts[3], indigenous and/or other mythological people are sometimes described as having a dark complexion[4], which carries with it this idea that the Picts/Pechts were not overly fond of direct sunlight either. In this same vein, the paler skin associated with *some giants*, might, I theorise, have to do with a lack of sunlight. So, although on a symbolic level, paler skin might be associated with a lack of sunlight, these pale skinned giants are certainly not the *only* mythological ancestors who seem to have an

3 *The use of the word Pecht is taken from Scottish mythology and is different from the archaeological and historical term Pict, which is in my opinion, much more limiting in definition.*

4 *An example in reference to the Pechts/Picts being of dark complexion can be found here:* *https://www.historic-cornwall.org.uk/the-picts-a-fierce-and-warlike-people/*

aversion to sunlight, as there are many that are not pale skinned and others still that have no specific skin colour at all.

In conclusion, although red hair and pale skin *may* be consistent with peoples who were not exposed to direct sunlight, the dark complexion of the Pechts in Shetlandic mythology, and the general mythological associations regarding the Pechts not liking direct sunlight, and not going outside during midday, would seem to demonstrate that, even if paler skin is *somehow* connected to a lack of sunlight, that other ancestors described as having darker skin also are associated with a general dislike of sunlight. So whilst the pale skin and lack of sunlight connection may be indicative of something, we also have examples of other ancestors, not described as pale, who also do not appear to like direct sunlight.

Returning to the idea mentioned in Hopi history about the world once being wetter, this might also in some way help to explain why these giants in world mythology are often connected to water or watery places. This loosely follows a connection between giants and the sea, something that I have already talked about previously in relation to the *ciuthach* of Gaelic mythology. Some of my work regarding this can be found in some of my omniglot articles, as given in the references section. I talk about the association between the ciuthach and sea caves, and brochs—mysterious Iron Age structures that more or less block out sunlight. Were brochs perhaps built this way because their giant residents did not like sunlight?

While the Pechts are not giants, and instead are described as "small people". I feel that they are also connected to elemental powers in nature; so whilst the 'giants' may be specific and have specific associations, there are also sometimes connections between them and other ancestral beings. Some of the mythology about 'small people' or 'good people' in Irish and British mythology, carries an implication that certain ancestors 'became' smaller after leaving this world and going to the underworld. But this is also true of some legends associated with giants, and with other ancestors. Regardless, I feel that ancient giants and smaller people in mythology relate to archetypal principles about nature and the cosmos, and perhaps to similar patterns and geometry existing at different levels of 'size' in the universe. Of course, these are only my thoughts and whilst this idea of changing size, is present, I am unable to interpret what it might truly mean.

Earlier, I mentioned the words "**Fe, Fi, Fo, Fum**", that were reputedly said by the giant in the tale of Jack and the Beanstalk. This is one example of a potentially more onomatopoeic speech with sacred meaning associated with these giant beings. Another example is reported from the Llŷn Peninsula in North Wales, where the *Tylwyth Teg* (a Welsh term for the little people) is thought to say **wi** (42) and is answered by the reply **wi wei** (42). So there is arguably something that connects this idea of pre-language or geometric language, to beings like giants and little people, and in a wider sense to gods and spirits.

However, I think it would be incorrect to try and explain the language similarities as coming from giants, because whilst giants and other beings might be associated with these ancient rhythms of geometric syllables and words, the possible physical aspects to these giants are I think only a part of the phenomena, the phenomena as a whole is I think far more connected to an inherent metaphysics related to refraction and to water within human history, than it is to any specific group of beings. Which might be why for example the megaliths on Shetland are connected generally to **Pechts** who are of small stature, and those in the Basque country may be connected to the **Basajaun** and **Basajaunes**, hairy beings of large stature. In a sense I feel that these beings such as giants, and little people, whether taken symbolically or literally, are 'closer' to the waters than we are, and that, like the **Apkallu** for example, they can be archetypal intermediators in relation to the process of refraction and wave-collapse upon which I have previously expounded. Similar ancestors or deities *may* be associated with similar traits in how languages have become independently developed by humans today, which is similar in a sense to my comment earlier about why the ancient Egyptians and Incas (and their predecessors) may have shared specific similarities in the knowledge conveyed through words and architecture.

A further comment regarding the connection between ancestors and water in relation to giants, might be found in the reports of some giant skeletons having two rows of teeth. If these beings were somehow more connected to water, two rows of teeth might be better suited to a diet high in shellfish which relates to my comment regarding the Omniglot article given as reference (46) and the shell food found at broch sites in Scotland.

Lastly, a very interesting connection can be seen in Shetlandic mythology regarding the Finns where they are again sometimes described as having a dark complexion and being of short stature.

The Finns in Shetlandic mythology are connected to the sea, and to magical power involving the sea, implying some ability for these ancestors to use words to physically manipulate matter, just as in other legends, giants are associated with having a magical ability to alter the physical landscape.

Furthermore, the Finns in Shetlandic mythology are connected to seals, and, throughout Scottish and Irish history, there is this idea of seals being some sort of ancestor beings, sometimes able to shapeshift into human form. This is also connected to the 'selkies' as they are known in parts of northern Scotland. This concept of magical beings coming from the sea in the form of seals, is clearly very old in Scotland. At the Cnoc Coig shell midden, archaeologists have found human bones buried in association with those of a seal (44); which leads this topic back to shell middens again and their potentially important symbolism.

Concluding Remarks

In concluding my comments on the various topics mentioned in this book and the possible connections between Indigenous American languages and other languages of the world, I feel it is important for me to again reiterate this idea of independent development. While some indigenous American cultures and languages may have some things in common with other cultures and languages, for hundreds of years, people largely of European descent have attempted to characterize these similarities as having been brought to the Americas from elsewhere. Unfortunately, this entire topic of human origins is often permeated by an apparent need to view some symbols, ideas, and cultures as being more important than others. But I do not believe this, I believe that the indigenous American peoples are from the Americas, and not from elsewhere, and that their incredible architectural and other cultural innovations are entirely their own. However, I do believe that the connections between the Americas and elsewhere are due to a collective, shared knowledge that all of humanity inherits in different ways.

In a sense, I think that human language and culture is like a grand library, with each culture and language having its own books. Perhaps what some have done in the past, is due to the fact that they have only been familiar with the Egyptian and European sections of that library, and so have assumed that any similarities found in Indigenous language and culture must have 'come from' the European or Egyptian sections of the this metaphorical library. And for this reason, many might ignore all the other thousands of books in the indigenous American sections which bear no similarity to others and are wholly unique to the Americas.

To carry this metaphor a bit further, I, on the other hand, am of the opinion that every single book in that library is equally important, and that we have to pay attention to what all peoples and cultures have to offer, in order to understand the library as a whole.

I hope that this was interesting to read, and that it in some small way honours all of the world's indigenous people.

References:

The number after a particular word and its translation indicates the reference.

(1) - Kichwa-English-Spanish Dictionary, by Nina Kinti-Moss Nematni Baltazar Masaquiza Chango, 2nd edition

(2) - Leslie G. Pride and Kitty Pride. 2023. Chatino (Zacatepec variety) dictionary.
In: Key, Mary Ritchie & Comrie, Bernard (eds.)
The Intercontinental Dictionary Series.
Leipzig: Max Planck Institute for Evolutionary Anthropology.
(Available online at http://ids.clld.org/contributions/223, Accessed on 2023-03-11.)

(3) - Kate Lynn Lindsey and Bernard Comrie. 2020. Ende (Papua New Guinea) dictionary. In: Key, Mary Ritchie & Comrie, Bernard (eds.) The Intercontinental Dictionary Series. Leipzig: Max Planck Institute for Evolutionary Anthropology.
(Available online at http://ids.clld.org/contributions/842, Accessed on 2023-03-11.)

(4) – Proto-Afro-Asiatic vocabulary is by Alexander Militarev, and Olga Stolbova, available on starlingdb.org, database by S. Starostin. Olga Stolbova has done a lot of work on Chadic languages, also the Chadic Lexical Database project.

(5) - Martine Delahaye. 2023. Tehuelche dictionary.
In: Key, Mary Ritchie & Comrie, Bernard (eds.)
The Intercontinental Dictionary Series.
Leipzig: Max Planck Institute for Evolutionary Anthropology.
(Available online at http://ids.clld.org/contributions/310, Accessed on 2023-03-11.)

(6) - Elena L. Najlis. 2023. Selknam dictionary.
In: Key, Mary Ritchie & Comrie, Bernard (eds.)
The Intercontinental Dictionary Series.
Leipzig: Max Planck Institute for Evolutionary Anthropology.
(Available online at http://ids.clld.org/contributions/311, Accessed on 2023-03-11.)

(7) - Ana María Guerra Eissmann. 2023. Yagán dictionary.
In: Key, Mary Ritchie & Comrie, Bernard (eds.)
The Intercontinental Dictionary Series.
Leipzig: Max Planck Institute for Evolutionary Anthropology.
(Available online at http://ids.clld.org/contributions/315, Accessed on 2023-03-11.)

(8) - Elizabeth Richards and Timothy Curtis. 2023. Lengua dictionary.
In: Key, Mary Ritchie & Comrie, Bernard (eds.)
The Intercontinental Dictionary Series.
Leipzig: Max Planck Institute for Evolutionary Anthropology.
(Available online at http://ids.clld.org/contributions/300, Accessed on 2023-03-11.)

(9) - Katherine Hall. 2023. De'kwana dictionary.
In: Key, Mary Ritchie & Comrie, Bernard (eds.)
The Intercontinental Dictionary Series.
Leipzig: Max Planck Institute for Evolutionary Anthropology.
(Available online at http://ids.clld.org/contributions/174, Accessed on 2023-03-11.)

(10) - Aikhenvald, A. (2002). Language contact in Amazonia. Oxford University Press. Accessed from DiACL, 9 February 2020.

(11) - Jorge A. Gómez Rendón. 2009. Imbabura Quechua vocabulary.
In: Haspelmath, Martin & Tadmor, Uri (eds.)
World Loanword Database.
Leipzig: Max Planck Institute for Evolutionary Anthropology, 1319entries.
(Available online at http://wold.clld.org/vocabulary/37, Accessed on 2023-03-22.)

(12) - Mary Ritchie Key. 2023. Tsimshian dictionary.
In: Key, Mary Ritchie & Comrie, Bernard (eds.)
The Intercontinental Dictionary Series.
Leipzig: Max Planck Institute for Evolutionary Anthropology.
(Available online at http://ids.clld.org/contributions/229, Accessed on 2023-03-22.)

(13) - Christos Clairis and José Pedro Viegas Barros. 2023. Qawasqar dictionary.
In: Key, Mary Ritchie & Comrie, Bernard (eds.)
The Intercontinental Dictionary Series.
Leipzig: Max Planck Institute for Evolutionary Anthropology.
(Available online at http://ids.clld.org/contributions/313, Accessed on 2023-03-11.)

(14) - Gildea (2007, 2012):

   1. Gildea, S. & Payne, D. (2007). Is Greenberg's "Macro-Carib" viable? In Boletim do Museu Paraense Emílio Goeldi. Ciências Humanas, Belém, Vol. 2, No. 2, pp. 19-72. Accessed from DiACL, 9 February 2020.

   2. Gildea, S. (2012). Linguistic studies in the Cariban family. In Campbell, L. & Grondona, V. (eds.), The Indigenous Languages of South America: A Comprehensive Guide. 441-494, Berlin: De Gruyter Mouton. Accessed from DiACL, 9 February 2020.

(15) - Booker, Karen. (2005). "Muskogean Historical Phonology." In Hardy, Heather Kay and Scancarelli, Janine (eds.), Native languages of the Southeastern United States, 246-298. Lincoln: University of Nebraska Press

(16) - Hewson, John. 2017. *Proto-Algonquian online dictionary*. Algonquian Dictionaries Project.
   • John Hewson. 1993. *A computer-generated dictionary of proto-Algonquian*. Gatineau – Quebec: National Museums of Canada. 281 p. ISBN: 0-660-14011-X
   • Hewson, John. 2001. The comparative method applied to Amerindian: the reconstruction of Proto-Algonkian. In *History of the Language Sciences*, eds Sylvain Auroux, E.F.K. Koener, Hans-Joseph Niederehe & Kees Veersteegh: Vol. 2:1384-1391. Berlin & New York: Walter de Gruyter.
   • Hewson, John. 2010. Sound change and the comparative method: the science of historical reconstruction. In *The Continuum Companion to Historical Linguistics*, eds Silvia Luraghi & Vit Bubenik, pp. 39-51. London & New York: Continuum.

(17) - Hewson, John. 1978. Beothuk Vocabularies. (Technical Papers of the Newfoundland Museum, 2.) St. John's: Newfoundland: Newfoundland Museum. 178Pp

(18) - Dimmendaal, Gerrit Jan. 1988. "The lexical reconstruction of proto-Nilotic: a first reconnaissance." Afrikanistische (AAP) 16: 5-67.

(19) - Ramirez, Henri (2019). Enciclopédia das línguas arawak: acrescida de seis novas línguas e dois bancos de dados

(20) - M. Catherine Peeke. 2023. Waorani dictionary.
In: Key, Mary Ritchie & Comrie, Bernard (eds.)
The Intercontinental Dictionary Series.

Leipzig: Max Planck Institute for Evolutionary Anthropology.
(Available online at http://ids.clld.org/contributions/255, Accessed on 2023-03-22.)

(21) - José Pedro Viegas Barros and Rodolfo M. Casamiquela. 2023. Gününa Küne dictionary.
In: Key, Mary Ritchie & Comrie, Bernard (eds.)
The Intercontinental Dictionary Series.
Leipzig: Max Planck Institute for Evolutionary Anthropology.
(Available online at http://ids.clld.org/contributions/312, Accessed on 2023-03-22.)

(22) - Mary Ritchie Key. 2023. Upper Chehalis dictionary.
In: Key, Mary Ritchie & Comrie, Bernard (eds.)
The Intercontinental Dictionary Series.
Leipzig: Max Planck Institute for Evolutionary Anthropology.
(Available online at http://ids.clld.org/contributions/232, Accessed on 2023-03-22.)

(23) - Kirk, Paul Livingston. 1966. Proto-Mazatec phonology. Ph.D. Dissertation. University of Washington.

(24) - Misión Nuevas Tribus. 2023. Pacaas Novos dictionary.
In: Key, Mary Ritchie & Comrie, Bernard (eds.)
The Intercontinental Dictionary Series.
Leipzig: Max Planck Institute for Evolutionary Anthropology.
(Available online at http://ids.clld.org/contributions/286, Accessed on 2023-03-22.)

(25) - Gerald Raymond Kennell, Jr.. 2023. Catuquina dictionary.
In: Key, Mary Ritchie & Comrie, Bernard (eds.)
The Intercontinental Dictionary Series.
Leipzig: Max Planck Institute for Evolutionary Anthropology.
(Available online at http://ids.clld.org/contributions/278, Accessed on 2023-03-22.)

(26) - María Clotilde Chavarría Mendoza. 2023. Ese Ejja (Huarayo) dictionary.
In: Key, Mary Ritchie & Comrie, Bernard (eds.)
The Intercontinental Dictionary Series.
Leipzig: Max Planck Institute for Evolutionary Anthropology.
(Available online at http://ids.clld.org/contributions/275, Accessed on 2023-03-22.)

(27) - Andrés A. Pérez Diez. 2023. Mosetén dictionary.
In: Key, Mary Ritchie & Comrie, Bernard (eds.)
The Intercontinental Dictionary Series.
Leipzig: Max Planck Institute for Evolutionary Anthropology.
(Available online at http://ids.clld.org/contributions/271, Accessed on 2023-03-22.)

(28) - Mary Ritchie Key. 2023. Mashco Piro dictionary.
In: Key, Mary Ritchie & Comrie, Bernard (eds.)
The Intercontinental Dictionary Series.
Leipzig: Max Planck Institute for Evolutionary Anthropology.
(Available online at http://ids.clld.org/contributions/264, Accessed on 2023-03-22.)

(29) -Foley, William A. (2018). "The languages of Northwest New Guinea". In Palmer, Bill (ed.). The Languages and Linguistics of the New Guinea Area: A Comprehensive Guide. The World of Linguistics. Vol.4. Berlin: De Gruyter Mouton. pp.433–568. *ISBN978-3-11-028642-7.*

(30) - Basque etymology Compiled by John Bengtson, available at: available on starlingdb.org, database by S. Starostin

(31) - Odile Renault-Lescure. 2009. Kali'na vocabulary.
In: Haspelmath, Martin & Tadmor, Uri (eds.)
World Loanword Database.
Leipzig: Max Planck Institute for Evolutionary Anthropology, 1373entries.
(Available online at http://wold.clld.org/vocabulary/38, Accessed on 2023-03-22.)

(32) - Søren Wichmann, Kerry Hull. 2009. Q'eqchi' vocabulary.
In: Haspelmath, Martin & Tadmor, Uri (eds.)
World Loanword Database.
Leipzig: Max Planck Institute for Evolutionary Anthropology, 1995entries.
(Available online at http://wold.clld.org/vocabulary/34, Accessed on 2023-03-22.)

(33) - Adams, Douglas Q. (2013), "taṅkw", in A Dictionary of Tocharian B: Revised and Greatly
Enlarged (Leiden Studies in Indo-European; 10), Amsterdam, New York: Rodopi, →ISBN, page 29

(34) - Douglas Q. Adams. 2023. Tocharian A dictionary.
In: Key, Mary Ritchie & Comrie, Bernard (eds.)
The Intercontinental Dictionary Series.
Leipzig: Max Planck Institute for Evolutionary Anthropology.
(Available online at http://ids.clld.org/contributions/209, Accessed on 2023-03-24.)

(35) - Douglas Q. Adams. 2023. Tocharian B dictionary.
In: Key, Mary Ritchie & Comrie, Bernard (eds.)
The Intercontinental Dictionary Series.
Leipzig: Max Planck Institute for Evolutionary Anthropology.
(Available online at http://ids.clld.org/contributions/210, Accessed on 2023-03-24.)

(36) - A Guanche vocabulary list by Alonso de Espinosa in the 16th century, as edited and
translated by Clements Robert Markham (1907)

(37) - Bach, Emmon. "MAKING SENTENCES", http://people.umass.edu/ebach/ehgrammr.htm

(38) - dictionary of Kallawaya created by Katja Hannß

(39) - Constenla Umaña, Adolfo (1981). *Comparative Chibchan Phonology*. Ph.D. dissertation,
Department of Linguistics, University of Pennsylvania, Philadelphia.

(40) - Félix Layme Pairumani. 2023. Aymara dictionary.
In: Key, Mary Ritchie & Comrie, Bernard (eds.)
The Intercontinental Dictionary Series.
Leipzig: Max Planck Institute for Evolutionary Anthropology.
(Available online at http://ids.clld.org/contributions/269, Accessed on 2023-03-29.)

(41) – Dravidian Vocabulary by George Starostin, available on this website https://starlingdb.org/

(42) - Story two, the Llŷn's Tylwyth Teg, available here on the Rhiw website:
https://www.rhiw.com/chwedlae/Tylwyth_Teg/tylwyth_teg2.htm

(43) - https://pantheon.org/articles/f/finn-folk.html (Encyclopedia Mythica)

(44) - https://www.digitscotland.com/a-load-of-old-rubbish-what-middens-can-reveal-about-
scotlands-past/

(45) - Klar, Kathryn Ann. (1977). Topics in Historical Chumash Grammar. Berkeley, CA: University
of California at Berkeley.

(46) - https://omniglot.com/language/articles/gaelicdialects.htm – Three Scottish Gaelic dialects and their possible relationship to ancient history, Linden Alexander Pentecost

(47) - https://omniglot.com/language/articles/ancientlanguage.htm - Ancient language and extra-Indo-European language in Britain, Linden Alexander Pentecost

(48) - https://omniglot.com/language/articles/ardnamurchan.htm Gaelic, and ancient language on Ardnamurchan and Rùm, Linden Alexander Pentecost

References (for Possible connections between Chimakuan, Celtic and Afro-Asiatic languages):

(1) – Proto-Afro-Asiatic vocabulary is by Alexander Militarev, and Olga Stolbova, available on starlingdb.org, database by S. Starostin. Olga Stolbova has done a lot of work on Chadic languages, also the Chadic Lexical Database project.

(2) - Sino-Tibetan etymology Compiled by Sergei Starostin, available at *https://starlingdb.org/* (same website as source 1)

(3) - Klar, Kathryn A. 1977. Topics in Historical Chumash Grammar. Doctoral dissertation, University of California at Berkeley.

(4) - Kaufman, Terrence (2017). Aspects of the lexicon of proto-Mayan and its earliest descendant. In: Judith L. Aissen, Nora C. England, and Roberto Zavala Maldonado (eds). The Mayan languages, 62-111. Routledge language family series. New York: Routledge

(5) - Booker, Karen. (2005). "Muskogean Historical Phonology." In Hardy, Heather Kay and Scancarelli, Janine (eds.), Native languages of the Southeastern United States, 246-298. Lincoln: University of Nebraska Press

Final notes:

As mentioned at the bottom of page 1 of this book, the title page (page 2 is the contents page), I hope to publish further etymological comments on Quechua in a new article, including some linked with Basque, which are not included in this book, because I discovered them after writing this book and its content, but before making the final edits and re-uploading on the 22nd of April 2023. This book does contain some comments on connections with Basque words as you will have seen, on pages 10, 11, 12, 14 (a total of 4 Basque words in addition to one Proto-Basque word are included/discussed, and a reference to Basajaun and Basajaunes on page 25), but the new article will contain some more, and further comments on etymologies more connected to Celtic.As I mentioned earlier, the etymological links included in this book are far from the only such etymologies I have found, most of those in this book I found only within the past few months. The omniglot article will also contain new etymologies not previously published. As mentioned on page one, I have also published a separate new book on giants in the Old North and in Wales, which includes some things on ancient language too. I published Old North and Wales giants book literally days after publishing this one, and although I technically published this book before the Old North and Wales book, I have added some edits to this book (Possible connections between Indigenous American languages and languages elsewhere, with particular reference to Quechuan languages, and with comments on elongated skulls, pyramids, giants and other philosophical points) on the 15th of April til the 22nd of April, whereas the Old North and Wales giant book was published on the 14th of April.

Printed in Great Britain
by Amazon

21835397R00018